# Motherhood My Way: Becoming a Single Mother by Choice

Dr. Regina A. Bailey

Copyright © 2018 Dr. Regina A. Bailey

All rights reserved.

ISBN: 1722794607
ISBN-13: 978-1722794606

# PROLOGUE

This is the story of my journey of why and how I became a single mother by choice.

What exactly is a single mother by choice or choice motherhood? It is when a woman decides she wants to have a child, wants to do it on her own and has a child using a sperm donor or sometimes through adoption. I had so many people ask me questions about why I did this, how I did it, what was the process, so I decided to write a book about it. In addition to answering those questions, hopefully it will also help other women that may be considering this path to motherhood.

## Decisions

Choice motherhood was never something I even considered until my 30's. I always thought I would have a "traditional family," get married, then have kids. But I put my career first and starting on a family on the back-burner. Some say I was too focused on my career, that is up for debate. I was a lawyer for 3 years before switching careers, went to medical school and after graduation from medical school spent many years in post-graduate residency training to become an Emergency Medicine Doctor. But around my mid-thirties I realized that I really wanted kids and I wasn't even close to doing it the "traditional" way.

So, after turning 36, and breaking up with my significant other (after he ignored my birthday and graduation from a master's program), I decided that I wanted to try to have a family on my own. On top of that, relationships were hard for me after being raped the year prior, and I didn't see that as something that was going to improve any time soon. This wasn't just a decision made on a whim. I thought hard, but I finally decided, it was now or never. My fertility was declining, I didn't want to put myself or my future child at any more risk because I had not met "mister right" or because I met mister right at the wrong time. I wanted to be a mom, I wanted a child.

My mother was also chronically sick; she had a heart attack, stroke, eventually was started on dialysis. She said her dying wish was to see a grandchild. She was always super traditional and strict (I wasn't even allowed to drive or date in college), but at that time in my life, she felt that this was a good idea. She was also worried that she would die, and I wouldn't have any close family; she just wanted me to have a family of my own before she died. After I made this decision she seemed to have something to live for.

So, after a lot of thought and discussion, I decided to do more research on IUI (Intrauterine Insemination) and to search for a doctor. After my visit to the RE (Reproductive Endocrinologist) and subsequent fertility testing, I learned that I had two key issues. First, based on the lab work and my age, even if I wanted to have children the "old-fashioned way," it likely would not have happened naturally. Second, because of trauma that occurred when I was raped one-year prior and scar tissue that subsequently developed, anatomically I could not have gotten pregnant the old-fashioned way either.

I also started the search for a sperm donor. Being that I lived in one of the largest cities in the country, I thought that this would be easy. Guess what? At the time, Houston did not have any sperm banks! The closest one was Austin. I searched the online profiles of the Austin sperm donors but did not see what I was looking for. My major criteria were someone that I may have dated in life and may had a child with. Education was also at the top of the list as well. Race was not a concern.

I ended up expanding my search to Los Angeles, Boston and New York City. I ended up finding my donor in New York. He was from South America, was an Attorney and wrote a beautiful letter as to why he was a donor. The online banks also provided baby pictures of the donors, as well as health information, blood type, grades, education, left vs. right handedness; they also do extensive screening for infectious diseases.

I ordered the sperm online and they shipped it directly to my doctor via FedEx. They had options of what type of sperm to buy (washed or unwashed, my doctor said unwashed was fine because his lab did their own washing), there is also options of quantity. Because of the cost of shipping the sperm (it must stay refrigerated to a certain temperature), my doctor recommended purchasing multiple vials so that if the first treatments didn't work, more sperm would be available. It cost several hundred dollars for a vial of sperm and shipping was a few hundred dollars as well. I would track the sperm online (it stopped overnight in Tennessee) and my mom and I would joke that we would nickname the baby FedEx because of how the sperm arrived in town. My mother never did look at the baby pictures of the donor (she said it made her too nervous, she didn't want to know).

## The Process Begins: IUI

So, I started medications to proceed with an IUI. I next took medications for a few days to help regulate my menstrual cycle and to help generate follicles. Days later, I had 3 follicles seen on ultrasound. I then did a trigger shot to trigger the ovulation of the eggs. Then on a specific day, I showed up and they injected the sperm into my reproductive system. I laid flat for about 30 minutes after the insemination and then I was free to resume my activities as usual.

The first IUI didn't work so I tried it again, that didn't work either. After the second failed IUI, my doctor recommended moving on to IVF (Invitro Fertilization) as he said I would have much higher success rates. After talking it over with my mother, I decided to give it a shot.

## IVF

The month prior to the IVF involved 2 weeks of taking birth control pills then starting medications by injections. The medications I injected would help stimulate my ovaries to create as many follicles as possible for retrieval. I meticulously gave myself injections daily for 2 weeks and 3-4 times a week I went to the doctor for blood work and ultrasounds. They would adjust my medications according to how my hormone levels were responding. A lot of times I would have to give myself and injection in the bathroom at work. It didn't bother me because I saw a bright light at the end of the tunnel, a baby.

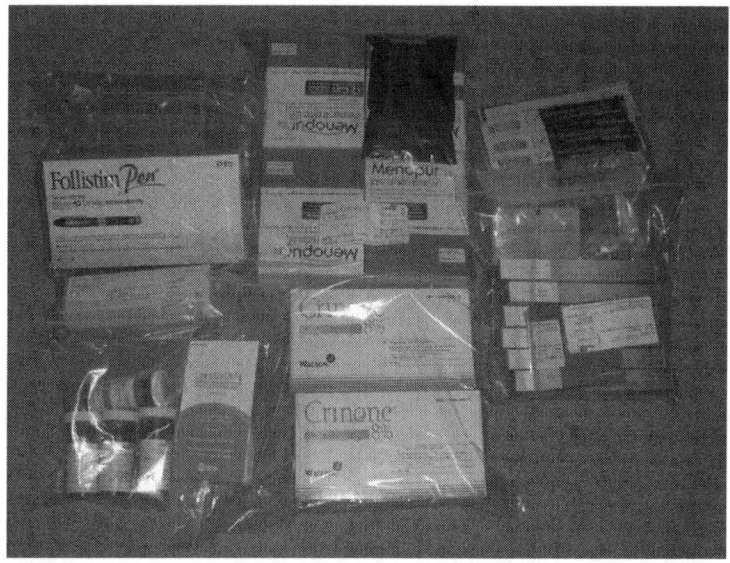

Finally, I had some good-looking follicles and had my retrieval done in November. The retrieval was done under anesthesia. When I woke up the doctor told me he was able to retrieve 13 mature follicles. Over the next few days those eggs were paired with the sperm and 10 of the 13 fertilized.

Five days later, the doctor transferred 2 of the best embryos into my uterus. The embryos were in a tiny syringe and the doctor would place them in my uterus with the guidance of an ultrasound. I watched the whole process on the ultrasound and he showed me the tiny bubble that were my embryos going in. The remaining embryos were frozen.

I went on 3 days of strict bed rest (I wasn't even allowed to shower). The reason for the bed rest is that after these procedures you are at a high risk of torsion and they also do not want your uterus to contract.

For the following days I hoped and prayed a whole lot, but 2 weeks later my pregnancy test was negative. I was devastated. I then found out that of my 10 remaining embryos, I only had 2 surviving the freezing process. I also learned that the lab was closing for the holidays for the last 2 weeks of December. If I wanted to transfer the frozen embryos I would have to take estrogen for 2 weeks, hope my lining of my uterus looked decent and pick a day to have them put in.

## I'm Pregnant

I went for it. In December I had 2 frozen embryos transferred and I went on strict bed rest again. I then went back to work. I was in my second year of Emergency Medicine residency at that time. That month I was working with an EMS crew and driving in trucks that at times were going 90 mph; I was doing chest compressions in the street and lifting patients. I thought, there is no way those embryos were going to survive.

Low and behold, 2 weeks later, I got a positive pregnancy test. I was so happy, I couldn't believe it worked! The first ultrasound showed 1 gestational sac and was measuring perfectly. They told me I would have to come in for ultrasounds and blood work twice a week. I didn't know how I was going to manage it with work, but I was determined to make it happen. The next ultrasound, surprise, 2 gestational sacs!

Over the next few weeks I watched my babies grow, took care of myself like I never did before (ate and drank healthy, rested whenever possible). I told everyone and did everything but shout from the rooftops, I was pregnant with TWINS! This was truly the happiest I have ever been in life and I couldn't really describe it. I marveled at the way my body was quickly changing. I once worried about gaining too much weight, but now I loved seeing my body expanding and growing, making room for those babies growing so rapidly!

## **Sadness**

At about 8 weeks gestation I learned that baby B wasn't going to make it but was assured that baby A looked perfect and would be fine. I was sad, but still hopeful since the other baby still looked good, I was still pregnant.

At around 10 weeks gestation, at what would have been my last RE appointment, the unexpected happened, baby A did not have a heartbeat. I was devastated, I loved those babies in a way that I had never loved anyone before. I would rub my stomach every day and tell them how much I loved them and would tell them to hang in there.

The next day I had a D&C. The D&C was done in the doctor's office with no anesthesia because I needed to be able to drive myself home. During the procedure the dilator got stuck in my cervix. I had a history of cervical stenosis and the doctor said this was the worst case he had seen in his medical career. My uterus started to contract around the dilator. They put me in a wheelchair and rolled me over to the hospital emergency room next door until an operating room was available to do the D&C under anesthesia.

After I woke up I remember crying and saying how much I missed my babies.

That night I still had a lot of pain and heavy bleeding. Two days later I had another D&C because there were still some retained products and my uterus was not reducing in size like it should have been. After the repeat D&C and the pain was just about gone and I physically felt better. Over the next few days my hormones were a mess and I was so depressed. I cried a lot, I felt like I had lost everything. At one time I even contemplated suicide, I felt like I had nothing to live for. Luckily, I had some good friends and a psychiatrist that helped me after my recovering from the rape help me through this tragedy as well.

## Renewed Hope

Finally, after about 2 weeks and after a follow-up appointment, I felt hopeful again. All was not lost. I was able to get pregnant and although short, I did get the chance to feel what it was like to be pregnant. I realized if I did ever get pregnant again, I would appreciate the experience and the baby so much more because of the loss. I think the experience made me a stronger person and, in the end, would made me a better mother.

After a lot of thinking, praying and talking with my mom, I decided to give the IVF another try. I quickly called the doctor's office to make my appointment for my blood work and ultrasound and they told me to come in the next day.

I went back to the doctor for a follow-up appointment, my ultrasound looked perfect, but unexpectedly, my betaHCG was still positive, I still had placental tissue or cells in my uterus. Because of that I could not start my cycle medications as I thought I would.

## Another Round of IVF

For the next two weeks my betaHCG levels were monitored (at this point it had been more than 6 weeks since my miscarriage). It had been trending down but was still elevated. I then finally got the all clear to start BCP's to start a new IVF cycle. Although my beta HCG was still positive, the numbers were low and trending down. I had a hysteroscopy done because of the multiple D&C's and because of the beta being elevated for so long, my RE just wanted to check to make sure everything was okay before starting a new cycle. He wanted to make sure I didn't have any small pieces of placenta left or scar tissue that may interfere with trying to pregnant again. Low and behold I had a lot of scar tissue. He was able to clear everything out and said I was all set to try again.

The next week I finally got the all clear to start BCP's to start a new IVF cycle. After 11 days of injection of stimulation medication, I got to do my trigger shot and 2 days later, I went in for my retrieval. This retrieval was done on a Sunday. Because the timing of IVF is so critical, the offices are open 7 days a week to accommodate this. It was weird being in a doctor's office in a

Sunday, but it was a lot more laid back and less stressful than usual. The doctor was able to retrieve 12 follicles. This retrieval seemed much easier than the previous; I had hardly any pain and bounced back quickly.

At that point, my eggs were having a date with a lot of sperm that night. The doctor's office called the next morning with the fertilization report. Out of the 12 follicles retrieved, only 5 fertilized. They still wanted to wait and do a 5-day transfer (transfer after 5 days of fertilization). I was so nervous since so many of my embryos didn't make it last time. When I originally heard the news I was upset, but then I thought that it only takes 1 embryo to have a baby and at least I still have a chance. I was praying the little guys keep growing and was looking forward to the transfer.

5 days after fertilization, they transferred 1 blast and 1 morula (I read up on morulas on the Internet and it sounds like they are like 1 day behind blasts). He said one of the two looked okay, but they weren't the highest grade they like to see. The other 3 embryos looked okay, but he didn't seem optimistic about their future (he said

"maybe" 1 would make it to freeze). It ended up that none of those embryos made it to the freeze phase.

My doctor started me on progesterone by mouth in addition to the suppositories, estrogen pills and patches and steroids as well; all medications to help support the transfer and support a potential pregnancy. I was placed on strict bedrest for two days (could only lay flat, no showering). The oral progesterone made me tired, so I did a lot of sleeping. I enjoyed the forced rest and relaxation (my body needed it).

A few days later I went back for my post transfer bloodwork. They said everything looked great and I just needed to keep continuing all the medications. I started to feel sleepy, nauseous and had bad indigestion (I know it was likely from all the medications, but I was secretly hoping they are super early signs of pregnancy). I had to go back a few days later for more bloodwork.

## I'm Pregnant Again

Even though I said I wouldn't, I took a home pregnancy test. I saw a faint line. I took two more the next day and still saw a faint line. I then searched the internet and found out the brand I used had a history of false positives, so I didn't want to get my hopes up (and didn't want to waste money on another home pregnancy test).

I held out and had my first beta HCG drawn (2 weeks after my 5-day transfer) and it was 443! I was so excited. I worried all day because my doctor's office didn't call until real late (they usually called early with good news, the doctor calls later in the afternoon if it is bad news). So, after I didn't hear anything by 3:00 I was convinced it was negative. Well, all the worry turned out to be a waste of time since the first Beta looked great. I was so happy and felt so blessed!

Twice a week for the next few weeks, I went to the doctor for blood work and ultrasounds. The baby was doing great. When the baby was about 9 weeks I saw it wiggling around. It looked like a dancing gummy bear and was the cutest and most heartwarming thing ever. At 10 weeks I officially graduated from the RE and could visit the regular Obstetrician for the rest of the pregnancy. I was so happy to make it so far and was so amazed that there was something growing inside of me that had a heart rate more than twice as fast as mine. I was so thankful to my doctor, his staff and most importantly God, for this blessing!

At 10 weeks 4 days I had my first regular OB Appointment. I heard the baby's heartbeat with doppler, I saw the baby move around again (it was rubbing its face then laid its arms over its chest).

Because of my family history of diabetes, they did the Glucola test (used to detect Gestational Diabetes) a few weeks earlier than normal. They also drew blood for the normal 1st trimester blood work. She also scheduled me for a NT scan (the Nuchal Translucency scan is used to detect physical abnormalities that may be seen) and blood work between weeks 12-13. The NT scan was to be done by a Perinatologist/Maternal Fetal Medicine (MFM) doctor.

2 weeks later I had had my NT scan done, the doctor said the baby looked great, was measuring 12w5d and he was 90% sure that it is a girl!!! As soon as my mother heard him say that she said "yeah, Fiona is coming."

At almost 18 weeks and had my second trimester ultrasound (my 11th ultrasound so far). They confirmed that the baby was a girl and looked great. My lab values from the 1st trimester screen put me in the high-risk category for Trisomy 13 and 18 and they suggested I get an amniocentesis. I declined the amniocentesis. With the amniocentesis there is a small risk of miscarriage. I thought it through and I could not put myself through the risk of the miscarriage. With it so difficult to get pregnant and miscarrying before I was too scared to do it. He said because the ultrasound didn't show any abnormalities that it lowered my risk some, so that gave me some comfort. They told me many times I had the option of terminating the pregnancy. The results were not going to change anything anyway. I already loved the baby, saw her face, and if she had some abnormalities that wouldn't change my love for her. The doctors continued to warn me of the risk that she may have one of those serious diseases (even up to the moment I was delivering her months later).

I also found out that my placenta was low-lying and anterior, and my cervix was short. The MFM was going to see me more often and said there was a chance I may need to get a stich placed (cerclage) to keep my cervix closed and even go on bedrest.

I started to feel the baby move around (felt like little flutters or like a popping sensation). Whenever I felt stressed out or down, feeling her always gave me comfort. Even though my belly was slowly getting bigger, it was still hard to believe there was a little one growing in there amazed me.

At close to 20 weeks I had another visit to the MFM. My cervix was still short, and he was worried it would get worse, so he decided to do a rescue cerclage the next day.

On a positive note, the baby looked great on the ultrasound. She had her leg kicked all the way up by her head and was covering up her ears with her little hands. My mom got a kick out of seeing the 3D pictures (it is amazing, how much you can see on there).

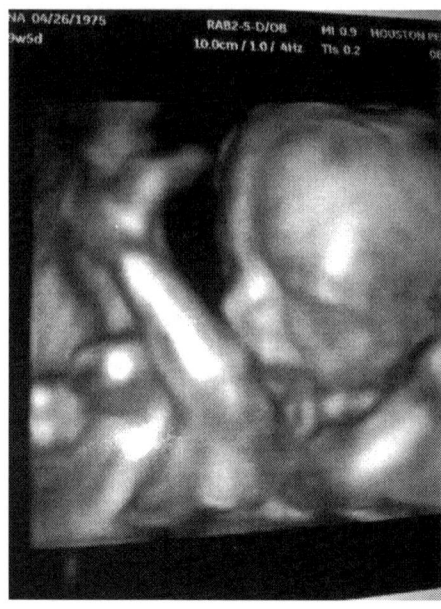

For the rescue cerclage, I had to have general anesthesia, so I was nervous about how it would affect the baby, however the baby recovered from the anesthesia faster than I did. She was up and kicking before I was even able to get up and walk around :-) The doctor said he was glad he did the cerclage because the cervix looked a lot worse than he expected. I didn't feel bad after the surgery, but the next day I had bad back pain and leg pain (probably from the positioning).

At almost 23 weeks I had a rough day at work. I had a few contractions but didn't think much of it. Later that night I started to have contractions every 10-15 minutes. I called the on-call doctor who told me to go to Labor & Delivery. They put me on the monitors for a few hours, I had a few contractions when I got there, then they slowed down and stopped. The baby was doing great, kicking around like crazy. They sent me home and just told me to stay hydrated and "take it easy at work," yeah right. I still didn't feel 100%, but glad the baby was hanging in there.

I went to the MFM for my routine follow-up appointment, this was 23 weeks. The baby looked great as always but had her head down and now my cervix was even shorter, 1.9 cm (down from 2.6). The doctor said he was glad he put the cerclage in, because it would have been even worse if he didn't. He thought I should be on bedrest but didn't want to harm my career (didn't want me to miss so much time from work that I would have to prolong my residency). He suggested I try to go back to work and see what happens. He said if I start contracting again I will have to be admitted to the hospital. He also gave me some medication (albuterol by mouth) to take if I start having contractions. I continued to pray and keep my fingers crossed.

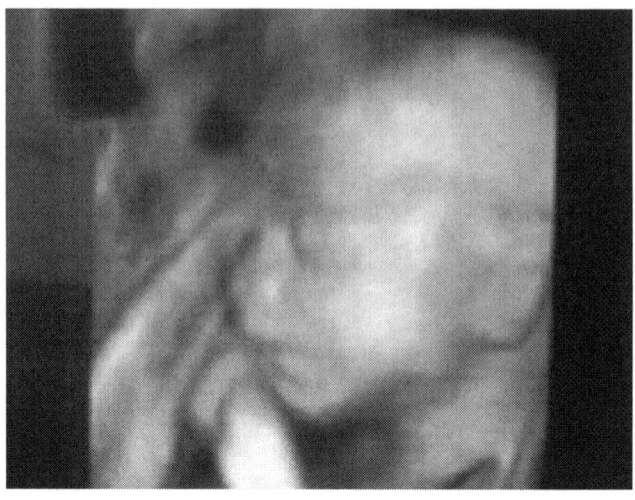

I went to the OB a few days later and was put on bedrest. I still had contractions every now and then, but the medication helped slow down. I was also started on progesterone injections to help keep my cervix closed. The baby was still moving around and doing great. They put me on the monitor for about 30 minutes. Fiona did not appreciate the tight belt around my uterus and continued to kick the belt from the inside...LOL. She moved around like crazy after I drank orange juice, ate sugary foods or if certain music was playing on the radio. I called her my little dancing queen.

The bedrest started to get me down (I had not left the house for 3 days), so I snuck out and drove my mother to the farmers market. It felt good to go for a ride, feel the wind blowing and the fresh air. I felt much better when I got home. I still got down here and there, but I realized I was healthy, the baby was healthy, and things could be a whole lot worse. I felt SO blessed that Fiona was in my life and made it so far (I was just hoping she could hold on a little while longer).

At this point in the pregnancy Fiona was wiggling around so much I could see her little head stick up out of my belly every few minutes, it was strange to see, but made it so real! She was such a blessing and made me so happy; I was so glad that she was becoming a part of my life!

I went for my next MFM appointment, I had reached 25 weeks. Everything looked stable, the baby was doing fine, but they were still real concerned that she would be a preemie. At that visit, I was given steroid shots; the steroids would help her lungs mature if she happens to delivered early. I asked the doctor how long he thought she could hang in there, he said a few weeks. I asked if he thought we would make it until 32 weeks and he said it was possible.

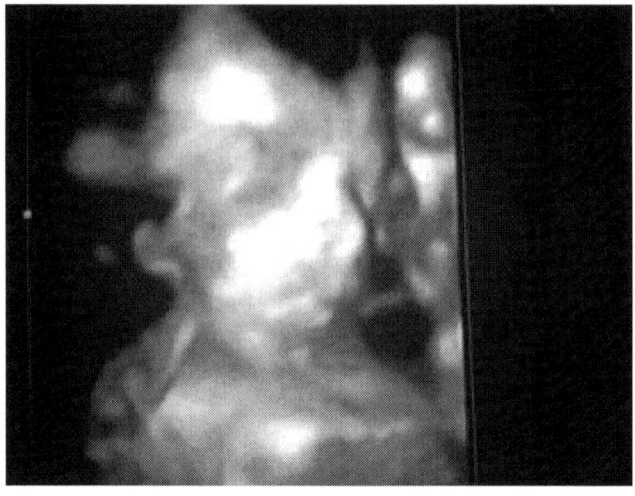

I went in for my regular OB appointment a few days later and she said to just hope for 28 weeks and explained that the NICU at her hospital has great success rates for 28 weeks and beyond. She said they really had no way to predict what will happen, she may stay full term, you never know. So, I continued with bedrest, and trying to keep her cooking!

At my next check-up I only had about 1 cm of cervix left, but it was still closed. The baby was still moving around like crazy and her heartbeat was holding strong in the 160s. The doctor still couldn't predict what would happen; I could have delivered any time or could go full term. So, we just kept with the status quo. I was so relieved to make it that far; I made it to the third trimester!

At my next MFM appointment, I was 29 weeks, the baby continued to look great, but her head was still down and pushing on my cervix. She was just as feisty as always (when the doctor pressed the ultrasound probe down on my belly, she punched it real hard-she hated getting poked). My cervix was still shortening (measuring 1.5 cm now and even smaller on exam), but I was still not dilating, which was good news. The doctor thought that I may be able to hold on to her for another 5-6 weeks, if I kept taking it easy.

I was also starting to finally get big, and with that also starting to get uncomfortable. It is all worth it though.

I had my regular OB follow-up appointment at 30 weeks, my cervix continued to shorten, but the baby was doing great. Again, they wanted me to continue the usual. I was complaining at the beginning of the pregnancy that I wasn't gaining enough weight; well low and behold, I gained 8 pounds in that past month.

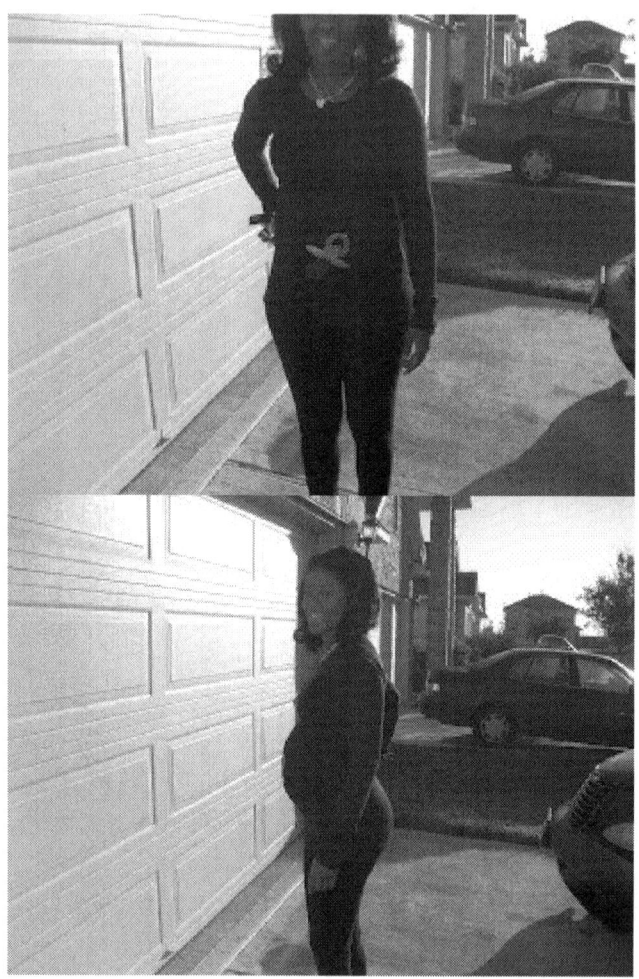

I continued with the waiting game, waiting to see when the princess felt like arriving. I started to get the nursery ready.

At this point (30 weeks), I had been on bedrest almost 2 months; just think at the start of the bed rest, I never thought I would make it to the 3rd trimester, let alone 30 weeks. I was so happy we got so far!

We made it to 32 weeks. Fiona was still growing well and looking great and weighed about 3.5 pounds per the ultrasound measurements. On her latest ultrasound she had her hand/arm covering her eyes and face, so we couldn't see what she looked like (I thought she was officially over all the ultrasounds and doctor's appointments). My cervix was holding stable, but I was having contractions here and there. Then my blood pressure started to elevate. Because of that they decided to increase my doctor's appointments to every week, and of course keep bed rest and all the medications. My butt was officially numb from all the progesterone shots, so they didn't even bother me anymore.

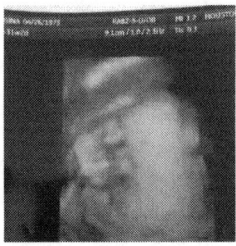

By this point, I finished her nursery; the bed was so pretty I wished I could sleep in it. I also finished putting together the pack and play, stroller and car seat. Physically I was all ready for her, but mentally was nervous. I couldn't wait to hold her in my arms and give her tons of hugs and kisses.

Around this time, I had used up all my FMLA time and no longer had an income. Luckily before starting the IVF process I signed up for sort term disability insurance. Being on bedrest during a pregnancy qualified as a short-term disability so I qualified and got some benefits from that.

The next few weeks were rough. I had bad contractions after Thanksgiving and had to go to the hospital twice. The first time they stopped the contractions with Terbutiline. The medicine made me feel horrible. They sent me home and an hour later the contractions started again. I went back to the hospital the next day and the contractions were so bad that they cut the cerclage out in the ER. They gave me some pain medicine and the contractions slowed down. The next morning, they stopped, and they sent me home. I continued to feel miserable but had made it to 37 weeks and was sooo happy to have made it so far. I couldn't wait to meet my little sunshine :-)

## Delivery

The next week I went to my OB for a routine visit and she decided to send me to the hospital to be induced. I was in labor for about 24 hours, it went smoothly, my epidural worked great and I had minimal discomfort. My mother stayed by my side the entire time. Of course, I had to go through all the questions again about where the father was, but I didn't care.

About the time I was fully dilated, I spiked a fever. They had to start antibiotics and now the NICU had to be present for the delivery. There were so many people in the room right before she was born, it was scary. I pushed a few times, I think the baby was in distress because the next think I know I felt pressure and heard scissors make a cut, my OB had done an episiotomy. I passed out and I guess she came right out. My doctor said open your eyes, she's tiny. She was blue and tiny, they rushed her out the room to resuscitate her but a few minutes later I could hear crying, and the nurse nudged me and said that was my daughter. Although she was a tiny 4 pounds and 11 ounces at 38 weeks, she was perfectly healthy. It looks like she had IUGR (Intrauterine Growth Restriction) and that is likely why I was having all the discomfort and contractions the month prior. Because of my having the fever she had to stay in the NICU to make sure she didn't have an infection. I only got to hold her for a few minutes before they scooped her away, but it was the best few minutes of my life. She was perfect in my eyes.

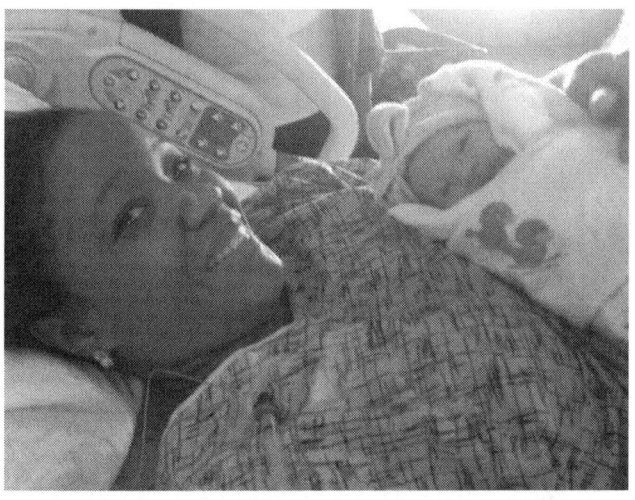

For the next day I would walk back and forth to visit her in the NICU. My mother had to leave because she was on dialysis and needed to go for treatment. I felt alone and emotional and cried often. Even though she was fine in the NICU, I still blamed myself for her being there.

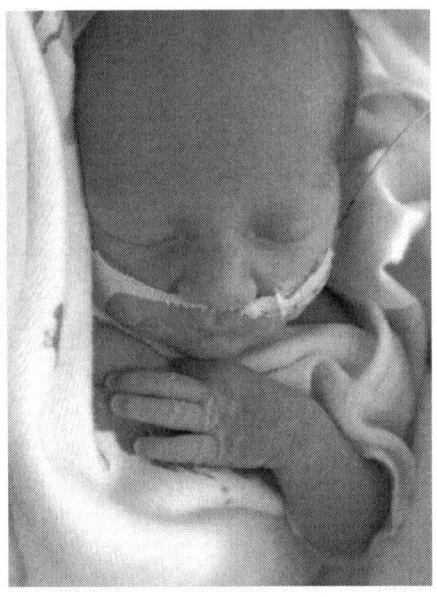

The next day I started to swell a lot and just wasn't feeling well. The staff wrote it off to me walking back and forth to the NICU so often, but in my heart, I knew something was wrong. That night my blood pressure was extremely high, and I was diagnosed with postpartum preeclampsia, was transferred to a different unit so I could be started on drips to control my blood pressure. The next day my blood pressure normalized, the doctors decided to discharge me (on no medications) and said that the placenta was the likely cause of the IUGR and the preeclampsia and now that my blood pressure was fine and the placenta out I didn't need to be on any medications.

As I was being discharged, my mother received a call from her transplant team that they found a potential donor for her, she needed to come to the Emergency Room to have some blood work done. So, I was discharged from the hospital, drove her to the Emergency Room and dropped her off until I heard back from her. Even though I just got out the hospital I knew I needed to go shopping because Fiona was getting discharged soon and I had no diapers or clothes that would fit her (I wasn't planning on her being so small, she was half the predicted weight they thought she would be so all the things I bought for her were huge). She was also going to have to be on special formula. So, after dropping my mother at the hospital, I went to pick up things to be ready for Fiona coming home. A few hours later, I got a call from my mother to come pick her up, they had someone higher on the list that they decided would get the kidney.

## Fiona Comes Home

Fiona did well in the NICU, only had to stay there a few days and was discharged home the day after I was discharged. The next day was Christmas Eve, I took my mother to dialysis, picked her up later and we went to get some food for the holidays. Suddenly I wasn't feeling well, I had a headache that felt like I could feel every blood vessel in my head throbbing and I saw flashing lights. I immediately knew what was wrong, my blood pressure, I still had preeclampsia. I managed to drive myself home, took my blood pressure and it was so high the machine couldn't read it. I was too scared to go to the hospital because I had no one to leave Fiona with (she was so small; my mother was too scared to hold her). So, I just took my mother's blood pressure medicine and tried to rest as much as possible. It was stupid on my part, but at the time I felt I had no other choice. That could have ended up bad, I could have had a seizure, stroke or even died. After Christmas I went back to my doctor that put me on medication to control my blood pressure.

Motherhood My Way: Becoming a Single Mother by Choice

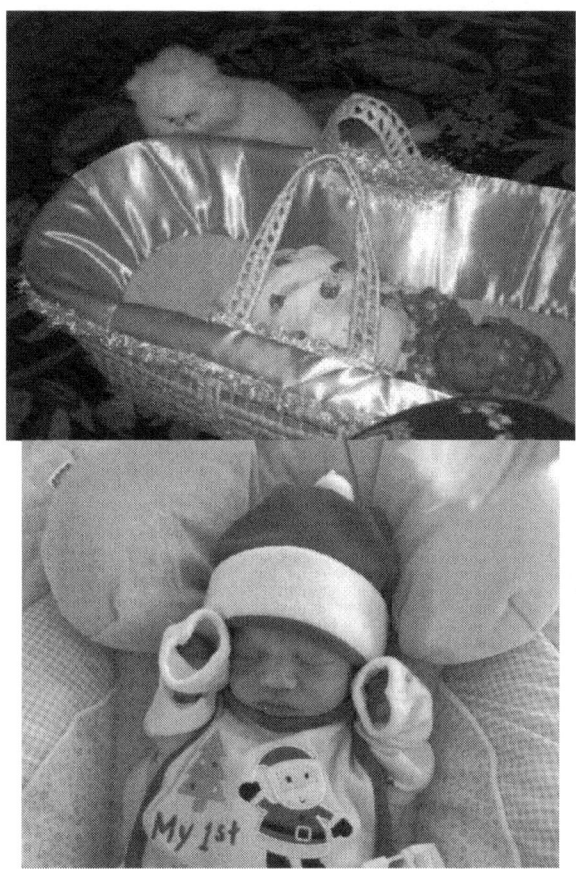

## The Early Years

The next 2 months were rough. Fiona had horrible colic and cried often. I found out that the local medical school had a colic clinic. I gave them a call and they gave me an appointment. They gave me tools like swaddling her better and using music to help soothe her and it worked. We ended up being on a story on the local news about colic and the colic clinic.

Once she hit 4 months she started sleeping through the night and life was so much easier. I was back at work. I would mostly work nights, so I could be there during the day and my mother would watch Fiona at night when she would be mostly sleeping. I was still a resident and, on that salary, could not afford childcare, so my mother watching her was a blessing. During the day I would take care of Fiona and drive my mother to dialysis and doctor's appointments. There is one important thing that I didn't account for in my plan, sleep, I had very little time for sleep. It took a toll on me, but we made it work.

About this time questions about Fiona started arising. When in public people would ask if she was my child, was she adopted, where she came from.

I wanted to have her baptized or christened, but my church didn't do that, and I had difficulty finding a church to do it (when they asked about the father and I told them, suddenly, the services weren't available to us). Eventually my father arranged to have her dedication at a church in New York that he did pro bono work for. It ended up being a beautiful service.

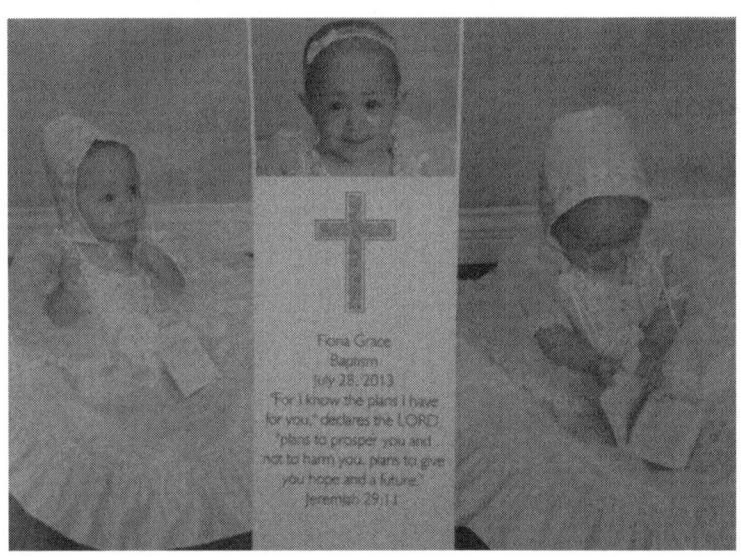

Fiona started taking ballet class when she was two. For her first recital, the dance school decided that they would have the daddies come on stage after her class was finished, present their daughters flowers and escort them off the stage. I freaked out and didn't know what to do. I asked my brother to come and act as the dad, but he didn't show up the day of the show. At the dress rehearsal at the time the dads came on the stage, Fiona looked around and fell out crying. I came on the stage to get her. Before the actual performance she had a meltdown, we almost left but her teacher convinced her to stay. During the performance later that day, when it was time for the dads to come on the stage, I stood up, walked towards the stage and Fiona screamed "that's my mommy." I presented her with a bouquet of flowers and she was all smiles.

For the next recital I thought the owners would see our dilemma and not do the daddy thing again, but they decided to do the same thing again. This time I asked my father to come to be on stage with Fiona. She was very excited and kept raving about how Grandpa came and got her on stage and brought her flowers.

Fiona and my mother were so close. They were buddies and even had their own inside jokes. But my mother eventually got too sick for me to take care of her anymore, I herniated a disc in my back lifting her and realized I couldn't do it on my own any longer. After suffering a subarachnoid hemorrhage from high blood pressure, she went to a rehab facility. Fiona and I would visit her just about every day and would have either lunch or dinner with her. We were there so often, Fiona befriended a lot of the residents there and often sang and danced for them.

When Fiona was 3 years old, my mother got very sick, unresponsive, was intubated in the hospital. She wasn't doing well, they didn't expect her to make it, so one of the doctors had one of the child life team at the hospital talk to Fiona about what was going on with grandma, showed her examples of the tubes she was hooked up to and demonstrated it on a doll and arranged to have her visit grandma in the ICU. Fiona held her hand, kissed her and said, "hi Mom-Gram." My mother opened her eyes for a few seconds and closed them-that was the most she had done during the entire hospital stay.

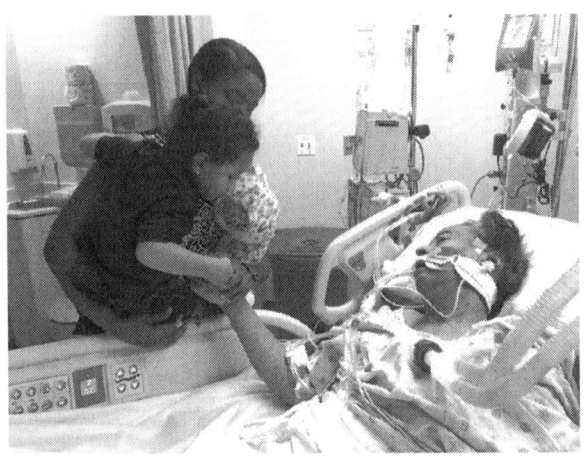

The next night I went to work and after I got off the night shift I went to visit her in the hospital. Everything seemed to be stable. After visiting for a few hours, I decided to go home to take a nap and come back later. A few hours later I received a call that my mother was coding and the doctors were trying to resuscitate her. By the time I made it back to the hospital, she had passed away. I was glad Fiona got to see her before she died, and it seemed like she said her good bye to Fiona when she opened her eyes for those few seconds. It was as though she was staying she knew we were okay without her now, she was tired and in a lot of pain.

My mother and Fiona were so close. Even though she was little she understood what happened, and at the funeral she went and kissed Mom-Gram on the cheek and touched her hair and told her she would miss her.

Fiona would ask to go to the cemetery frequently to visit Grandma-for some reason after she was buried Fiona didn't call her Mom-Gram anymore, she called her Grandma. She would always ask to get flowers to bring to the cemetery, she would arrange the flowers herself, bring pictures and clean the grave site. She said the cemetery was the place where grandmas went when they got sick and that we visited there to remember them. She was young but understood it and handled it so well.

When Fiona was 4 years old, she woke up in the middle of the night crying. I asked her what was wrong, and she said that she wanted a daddy. She didn't ask why she didn't have a daddy, simply said that she wanted one. Kids at school were starting to ask her about her daddy and there were frequent discussions in school about families. I didn't tell her why she didn't have a daddy. But I did explain to her that not everyone had a daddy. That some kids have 2 mommies, some have 2 daddies, some have just 1 mommy and no daddy or 1 daddy and no mommy.

Around this time Fiona would also tell me that she didn't have a family. I told her that I was her family and kitty was too, and that although we had a small family, we were still a family. I also talked to her about her extended family. I always tried to discuss with her the positives about our small family. I also told her that with our small family we could afford to take more vacations, and if our family was larger, we could not afford to travel so much. It seemed to me like she wasn't buying it, but it was the best I could explain at the time.

My father passed away suddenly when Fiona was 5 years old. Again, she handled it very well, but she had a lot more questions about death and it gave me a wake-up call to my mortality as well. She asked me if I was going to die while she was still a kid and if I did, what would happen to her. This scared me too and I had many sleepless nights as had no good answers for her. I really had nothing prepared and didn't know what would happen to her if I died. I told her that we never know when we will die, but that I would make sure she was well cared for if I did die while she was still a child. It was time for me to get my affairs in order.

Father's Day was right after my dad died. At school they made paper ties for the dads and put them on a bulletin board that said, "Fathers tie our love together." I was expecting her to say something to me and I didn't know what to say. She didn't have a dad to give it to and I couldn't even tell her she could give it to grandpa. She didn't ask any questions, just showed me which one her tie and I told her what a great job she did making it.

That summer continued to be rough for me. I often would be the only one cheering her on at swim meets, recitals, cheerleading competitions, awards banquets. It really hit me hard early one morning when I was at a swim competition. Fiona was down because almost everyone else had a large family and a tent set up to have somewhere to relax while waiting for their child to swim. We were just there with our 2 lawn chairs and a small cooler. She asked why we didn't have a large family and why we didn't have a tent. I felt so alone at the time, I was always proud of her, but often wondered if she felt bad that she didn't have a large group of people cheering for her like most of the other kids did. After that I ordered a tent from Amazon and at the next swim meet I lugged the tent, chairs, coolers to the swim meet. I struggled, but managed to set the tent up, Fiona beamed. We may not have had a big family cheering her on, but we had our own tent (it was hot pink) and I was there to cheer her on. It was something small, but it meant the world to her.

## EPILOGUE

There are some things I wish people knew about choice moms, including myself. We are not strange or crazy. We are woman that love our children and wanted to have them so bad that we made the tough decision to do it on our own.

There are also things I wish people that see families that may not look like "traditional families" would stop doing. These are all things that people have asked me. Please don't ask who or where my child's father is front of my child. I have no problem discussing this with you privately, but I have not had that discussion with my child yet. Please don't ask what my child's race is in front of her or why she looks differently than me or what is the race of her donor. Again, this is a subject that I have discussed with my child yet.

People also ask if I made the right choice or if I would have done anything differently. I know I made the right choice. Fiona is truly the best thing that ever happened to me, she makes me a better person, brightens my day every day and I have learned so much from her. I have learned to enjoy sunsets, the moon, stars, flowers, these are all things I took for granted. I have learned to slow down and enjoy life, enjoy the little things. I have learned to not give up, to keep trying to push for my dreams. I have learned to be strong and fearless. These are all things I have seen her do and have learned to do myself. The only thing I wish I had done differently is perhaps had her earlier so that I could have had a sibling for her as well. At my age and with all the complications I had with my previous pregnancies, I would be at even higher risk to carry a child now (not to mention the difficulty conceiving with my 43-year-old eggs would bring as well). It would be too risky to have a child at this point, especially being single. If I was on bed rest again, it would be too difficult on Fiona.

I will never regret having Fiona, she is truly a blessing, but I do wonder if what I did was fair to her. Does she really need a father figure in her life? These are questions I still have not answered and likely will not be able to answer. But I do know that I will continue to raise her with as much love and support as humanly possible. I may not be able to be a dad, but I will be the best mom that I can to her.

I hope this book helps other women that may be considering this option, helps other non-traditional families and educates those that have questions about us. I also hope this book helps families that have been through IVF and/or miscarriage and hope that it gives them a ray of hope. There is no end to this book as our story is still in motion. We are still growing, learning and adapting as we go.

# ABOUT THE AUTHOR

Dr. Regina Bailey is an Emergency Medicine Physician, Lawyer, Fitness Expert, Former NFL Cheerleader, Beauty Queen, Best Selling Author, and Motivational Speaker.

Dr. Regina received a BA in Molecular Biology from Hampton University, JD from Georgetown University, MD from the George Washington University School of Medicine, and Masters in Health Law from the University of Houston Law Center.

Prior to attending law school, she did biomedical research at Yale University, Stanford University and the National Institutes of Health. Prior to attending Medical School, she was a patent attorney in Washington, DC where she fought for the rights of generic drug companies to get their lower cost drugs on the market.

She completed an Internship in General Surgery at University of Texas Health Science Center at Houston and completed Emergency Medicine Residency at the Baylor College of Medicine.

She has published books and articles in the health law, medical, biotechnology and Emergency Medicine fields. She speaks on the above topics, as well as medical school admission tips, fitness, surviving sexual assault, and choice motherhood. She has appeared on TLC, Discovery Life Channel, CNN, and the E! Channel. She has been published in the New York Times, US News, Medscape, Huffington Post and Ebony Magazine. During her free time, Dr. Regina she competes (and wins) pageants and fitness competitions.

Dr. Regina is CEO of "Fit and Fine in No Time" a company that provides, nutritional supplements, meal replacement shakes and weight loss products all formulated by herself.

Printed in Great Britain
by Amazon